Mountain Boy
Management Skills

By Raland J. Patterson

Every morning in Africa, a gazelle wakes up. It knows it must outrun the fastest lion or it will be killed. Every morning in Africa, a lion wakes up. It knows it must run faster than the slowest gazelle or it will starve. It doesn't matter whether you're a lion or a gazelle—when the sun comes up, you'd better be running.

Columnist Herb Caen

1
Introduction

If you're not having fun as a manager of people, then you're doing something wrong. As one of my mentors explained to me, there are three phases of working as a manager. The first is **the job phase**. This is when you're just learning your new occupation. In this phase you're so afraid the employee might ask you a question for which you do not have the answer that you approach each day with nervous anticipation. The second is **the career phase**. The best indicator that you have entered this phase is that you would give anything if only your guys would ask a question you haven't heard before. You look forward to each work day because you're building a great team. The third is the **"calling" phase.** You don't look at your occupation as a job or a career anymore, but as a deep-seated need to help everyone in your area of expertise. My career went through all three phases. Because my mentor had described them in great detail, I was able to recognize the transitions. Better still, I was able to help speed the process along.

Have you noticed how everyone is looking for the one thing that puts successful people on top of their respective professions? If that's what you are looking for, I can't help you. If there is just **one thing,** I was never smart enough to recognize it. What I can give you, after 20 years of successful entrepreneurship, is a list of things that will make the workplace more fun and improve your odds of hitting your business targets at the same time.

Why should inexperienced managers learn everything the hard way when my managers and I had found some solutions they might use?

My mission with this book is to assist new managers in identifying problems, recognizing the similarities to problems I encountered, and offering possible solutions to those problems.

I have selected a few anecdotes from my experiences to illustrate certain points.

Each one taught me a lesson--- not necessarily at the moment, but sometimes years later. (You could say I'm a slow learner.) It would be naïve of me to think that each of the stories will teach you something; however, they may stimulate your memory of other events that had a positive impact in your life and remind you of a particular lesson you learned from it. After all, **the school of hard knocks** is a pretty good teacher.

2

Corncob Fight

I recalled a number of stupid things I've done in my life. It is true that everyone makes mistakes from time to time, or participates in foolish acts. Nevertheless, one particular stupid decision I made as a child still bothers me as an adult, simply because I didn't feel my decision was stupid at the time. In fact, I felt inspired by my brilliance in discovering an immediate solution to my problem.

I was born and raised on a small 200-acre farm in northern Georgia. My family raised cattle, horses, pigs and corn. At one end of our meadow we had three haystacks, each rising approximately twenty feet in height. I had friends who lived "in the area" (I can't say neighborhood because city folks think in blocks). We thought in miles. However, I don't remember losing a lot of time worrying about walking to my friends' houses.

One afternoon my friends and I decided to have a corncob fight around those twenty-foot haystacks.

Once the corn was removed from the cob, the cob was very light. What this meant to the thrower was that the cob lost momentum and distance very quickly. The hitting distance, or "kill-zone", was twenty feet or less. Even at this short distance, healthy farm boys could quickly move out of the path of an on-target cob.

The problem as I saw it was that the corncobs were just too light. The next time we went to the corncrib to reload our arsenal, I was inspired with a solution that would increase the weight of the corncobs. I knew there were plenty of leftover corncobs in the pigpen. The difference between the cobs in the pigpen and the ones in the corncrib was that the cobs in the pigpen were wet! I knew wet cobs were heavy, and heavy cobs fly faster and farther. How's that for inspiration?

Fully loaded, we all moved back to our fighting positions. James was going to be my first victim because he was predictable. (You do not want to be predictable in a corncob fight.) Every time I threw a corncob that whizzed past him, he would immediately stick his head out from behind the haystack and throw his cob.

My plan was to lob a dry corncob underhanded with my left hand and then throw the wet one with my right. My plan worked. Just before the dry cob hit the ground, I hurled the wet cob as hard as I could at the place where James always stuck his head out. This time was no different; his head was exactly where I predicted it would be.

The cob hit James directly on the left temple, and he dropped like a rag doll. The other boys saw the blow and ran to James' side.

One announced, "I think you killed him!"

I was in shock. To make matters worse, James' entire body began to shake. At the time it reminded me of a chicken with its head cut off. The first thing that ran through my mind was: *How am I going to tell Daddy I killed James?*

Luckily, I never had to confess to corncob murder. James woke up, and he didn't even cry. All he said was, "Don't you go telling my mother!"

I stood there in a daze. I tried to relax and think about what my Dad would say or do. That was easy. He said the same thing every time I did something stupid: "Son, did you learn anything from this?"

My answer was always, "Yes, sir." In most cases I was glad he didn't ask me what I had learned because I didn't know. In this case the obvious answer to Daddy's question was, "**Don't hit your friend in the head with a wet corn cob.**" What I learned in a broader sense is that my first solution to a problem is not always the right one.

Later on, I realized this lesson applied to quick fixes in business also. I discovered that the quick fix was almost always wrong.

3

Rules and Laws

As I look back at my career, I can identify four rules that kept me on the path to success:

1. **Establish goals**
2. **Take care of your teams and friends**
3. **Don't get greedy**
4. **Don't fool yourself**

In my experience, if you do not have rules or standards to live by, even small decisions become major hurdles. I look at my four rules as a road map for life. I've spent over forty years in leadership or management positions. My leadership education started in the Army with nearly four years as a Company Commander. My soldiers had to follow my orders to the letter because I was their Commander; but it didn't take long to realize to be a good Commander I needed to listen and to delegate.

In other words, I needed to trust my soldiers to do their jobs. When I entered the business world I discovered quickly that civilians are looking for guidance and direction as well. I learned in the Army to be consistent and to maintain my focus. While in the Army, people's lives depended upon it. After 22 years of keeping watch I decided to try something else, and I retired as a Lt. Colonel.

I was excited when the company gave me the European Region to lead. For the first time I could practice all the leadership and management skills I had picked up over the years and observe the results. I established goals and gave expectations to my management team.

My major goal was to double the number of agents in five years – we made it in three. I expected my managers to lead by example. Retention of agents was paramount in meeting our goal. I offered stringent guidance in this area.

Retention – if a manager lost two agents because of lack of leadership it would result in a discussion as to whether the manager should step down.

a. Acceptable Losses – health, promotion, retirement.

b. Other losses fell into the category of poor leadership.

In the six years I led the region I only lost one manager for poor retention. Of the twenty-one regions in our company, we had the highest retention rate and the highest number of district agents promoted – 26.

In addition to my four rules I had my 12 laws. They helped me over the years to come to a decision a little easier. I chose to call them laws because like the law of gravity, you might violate them once in a while and get away with it; however, if you make a habit of trying to beat the law of gravity you will end up with your face in the dirt. As I got older, I learned to hate the taste of dirt. My laws help me to dine less often.

4
PAT'S LAWS

1. Cheap people cannot think big.
2. <u>The</u> yeses change our lives, not <u>the</u> no's.
3. Plan for success.
4. Successful people face more problems than unsuccessful ones. This is the reward for being successful.
5. You never desire anything you're not capable of doing. (If you're willing to pay the price).
6. If you don't mess up, you're not doing anything.
7. There are no bad goals, just bad timing.
8. Sharpening your tools is never a waste of time.
9. Knowledge is power only when you share it.
10. When you have problems, think horses not zebras.
11.

12.   Everyone has a 'clear bead' desire.

13.   Keep them hungry.

In the Army I was taught when teaching a class: Tell them what you are going to tell them. Then tell them. Then tell them what you told them.

You will also read about attitude, goal setting, team building, consistency, and communication.

5

Communication

I'd like to take credit for learning the importance of communication; however, that wouldn't be fair. The man responsible for this enlightenment was my Command Sergeant Major (CSM). When I was a young Captain about to take command of an eight-inch firing battery, which had just failed an ORTT (operational readiness training test), my CSM was eager to give me guidance. As I entered his office, he explained I had two options as a new Commander. I could be an easy-going, laid back one, or a nasty, foul-mouthed one. Either option would work – and had. Even if I was a nasty one, the troops would respond because I was "their" Nasty Commander. Then he told me what the most important part of this lesson was. "Whichever route you decide to take, make sure you're Consistent. You need to stay the course. Being consistent is the mark of a good Commander.

The soldiers expect it – in fact, they both deserve and expect it." The CSM went on to supplement my education. He first reminded me that the battery had failed the ORTT. This meant the unit was not combat ready. He warned me that they would be retested in the next couple of months. He didn't hesitate to identify what he thought was the problem. The Commander I had replaced was aloof. He thought he was too important to talk to his soldiers. In fact, most of them were afraid of him and didn't want to talk to him anyway. Then the CSM gave me the solution. "You have some of the best soldiers I've ever seen. What they need is for you to tell them what is expected of them and explain why. If they know the why, you will be surprised at how well they perform." He ended by saying, "No one likes to be a failure. They feel like failures now. Make them winners."

It would be an understatement to say I was pumped when I left the CSM's office. I explained to my First Sergeant what the CSM had suggested. I saw a little smile on his face. I didn't learn until I gave up my command one year later that he and the CSM had planned the entire thing.

When I asked the 1st Sergeant what I should do first, he was prepared for the question. He handed me a stack of reports almost an inch thick. These were the gig sheets on the last evaluation. The sheets listed the requirements, expectations and, worst of all, the battery's sub-par performance. It took me until two o'clock the next morning to read through them. The next morning I had everyone meet in the day room. It took me all day, but I read every page out loud. I answered any and all questions before we moved on to the next page.

What happened? I'll use one event to answer that. Six weeks after taking command the battery was retested. The test took three days to complete. The eight-inch firing battery was a mechanized unit. The Howitzers and the 548 ammunition carriers were track vehicles. As a commander, I traveled in a Jeep. During the evaluation the senior evaluator, a Major, rode with me the entire time. One of the areas in which we had failed miserably was Air Guards. The 548-ammunition carrier has a 50-caliber machine gun mounted on the front of the vehicle.

During convoys one of the crew was required to man the 50 cal. as long as they were traveling. His job was to watch for any enemy aircraft and return fire from an ambush. My battery was usually divided into two convoys – one with track vehicles and one with wheel vehicles.

Just my luck, when we moved to the field it began to rain. I'm talking about a Texas rain. As my brother says, a frog strangler. After a day of rain the wheel vehicles could no longer follow the track vehicles on the tank trail. My driver was forced to drive on the hard surface road. He would stop periodically on the highway so the evaluator could observe the battery as they moved up the tank trail. On the last day of the evaluation the driver had stopped to observe the convoy when the clouds really opened up. Water was running over the banks of the ditch on the side of the road. In a couple of minutes we could see the tracks coming. There were four Howitzers and four ammunition carriers in the convoy. The Major almost jumped out of the jeep when he saw that even in a downpour every gun mount had a soldier doing his job.

The Major looked at me and said, "Take me home, Captain. I've seen enough."

The following week our battery was awarded the "Best by Test" trophy. The CSM was right: communication was all my battery needed. Even in civilian life, I still tell, tell, tell. I tell everyone under my supervision my four rules, my laws, my goals, my vision and, most importantly, I tell them about their successes and accomplishments.

I feel the biggest mistake made by civilian managers is that they fail to take care of their people. In the Army my men knew I was there to take care of them and I had no doubt they would be there for me. Soldiers will die before they let their buddies down. If you've never worked in this kind of environment you have missed out on one of life's pleasures. As a leader, and I say that because in the Army I was taught you lead people and manage situations, I learned I had to take care of my people. I soon found out my actions spoke much louder than my words. But I must warn you that I also found that just like listening this can be extremely hard work.

As I mentioned before, a snap decision gets you into real trouble. I found when I made one of these snap decisions off the top of my head if it had an impact on one of my people the result was that it created an invisible wall between me and them. His perception of me was I was cold and callous and only looking out for myself. I quickly discovered that perception is fact in the real world and was surprised to find it was not the big things I did but the little ones that had the most impact. A box of candy or flowers in their room when they were on a company-related trip, publically recognized birthdays and anniversaries at meetings, a gift certificate for an anniversary dinner are all examples of making someone feel special.

Over the years I've learned the best and most powerful tool I had was expecting my team members to succeed. It always amazed me how quickly they would rise to my expectations. I stumbled on this technique as a National Guard Advisor. The unit leaders would tell me what their standards were, but when we went to look at the unit I could quickly see what their standards really were. Take a "Don't fool yourself" moment.

If you've been in charge for six months or more, do a system and team evaluation. What you'll discover is your real standards, not what you think they are. Good or bad, these are what you have settled for or achieved while leading your team.

Do you trust your people? If you don't trust them, how can you expect them to trust you? As my grandmother used to tell me, "If you tell the truth, you never need to remember what you said." Tell your people the truth, respect them and have high expectations. They deserve it. I found if you respect them and give them praise, they grow as a team. Over time I discovered that the most powerful statement you can make to a team member that is slacking off is, *I'm disappointed in you.* This statement is a major big stick, which I have used very sparingly. I tried to use the ratio of *50 praises* to your team for *one disappointment in you*. I say 50 because I found it takes that many or more to build self-esteem in them as a team. As you'll discover, very few people have been exposed to an awesome team. I learned it takes a while for them to adjust; but trust me, it's worth it.

6

The *Yeses* Change Our Lives, Not the *No's*

Loud crashes, ice-cold water on your face, or the sweet aroma of your favorite dinner are all things that get your attention. But have you ever heard a statement that stopped you in your tracks? "The **Yeses** change our lives, **NOT** the **NO's**" really hit home for me. A few years ago a bitter middle-aged man had just gone through a horrible divorce and sworn off women forever. His friends were always trying to fix him up with the perfect lady. Most of the time he would say no. He felt he knew better than they whom he wanted to be with, even if it was only a date. The truth was that the few blind dates he did accept turned out to be great. The ladies he approached himself turned out to be nightmare dates.

There is a heroine of the story. She, too, had gone through a bad divorce from a cheating husband. She had not sworn off men, but she did not think a man could be better than a good book by a warm fire.

Reading and work became her life. She worked from 3 o'clock in the morning until six in the evening. Truthfully, the only thing that came in second to reading and work was cooking. Her cooking was grand and proved to be a real talent.

On with the story. Her dentist had been trying to "fix her up" with different guys for almost nine years. The dentist and the bitter man were members of the same Kiwanis Club. The dentist knew just how empty the bitter man's and the heroine's lives were. The dentist's heart nearly stopped when the heroine said **YES** to a blind date. As soon as she left his office, the dentist called the bitter man and told him that a wonderful lady wanted him to call her right away. Really she had not, but the dentist was so afraid that if the man waited too long she would say no, as she had done so many times before. In fact, the first time the bitter man called her she did not want to meet him. She would not even let him know where she lived. Two months later the bitter man found her phone number in the pocket of his suit coat and tried again.

This time the call went better. She agreed (**YES**) to meet him at a neutral place. She described herself as a five-foot-six lady with gray hair.

The man arrived early and it seemed as if everyone else in town had chosen the same restaurant. Then a gorgeous lady came through the crowd. He could not see anyone else. He called her name, and she said that magic word, "Yes." One year later, in front of over one hundred people, she said "yes" again when he asked her to marry him. Because of **yes**, they are living happily ever after.

I hope this true story convinces you that the **yeses** are what change our lives. Let me remind you that we Americans are the luckiest people in the world. But we have been trained to say no. You don't believe me? What do 90% of people say when a saleslady approaches them in a store and asks? "May I help you?" We know that most are looking for something. Look for a reason to say **yes**. Or every time you say or hear a **no**, let that raise a **red flag**. Think about it. If the answer were yes, what might have happened?

7

Write It Down

Once upon a time a little boy was stricken with polio the summer after his third birthday. He was forced to wear a brace on his left leg and learn to walk again. He did this with a lot of encouragement from his Mom. Just before he started first grade he was able to shed the brace. As his leg improved he began to run and play as a normal child with only a slight limp. One day he announced to his Mom that someday he was going to learn how to dance. He thought if he could dance, no one would notice his limp.

As usual, his Mom was supportive. She didn't even hesitate as she said, **"Son, write it down so you won't forget."**

His Mom only had a seventh grade education but she knew instinctively that anything important had to be written down. This was the first time of many that the child heard he should write his goals down.

This simple suggestion from his mother proved to have a major impact on the little boy's life. Throughout the years he wrote down things so he wouldn't forget. He wanted to be a Second Lieutenant, run a marathon, learn to fly, play chess, own a sailboat, and write a book. I could go on and on, but it's not needed. However, goal getting is on the other side of the formula. He ran three marathons, flew helicopters over an active volcano in Hawaii, retired as a Lt. Colonel, won a chess championship while stationed in Korea, and was given a deal he couldn't pass up on a sailboat.

What about the dancing? He was awarded the "Most Agile" trophy at his 40th high school reunion. They declared him a dancing fool.

8

Establish Goals

Writing down your goals and reading them often can become a powerful tool. Why? This is the quickest and easiest way to let your subconscious know what you really want. You may not realize it, but the subconscious has no sense of humor. If you think you can or think you cannot, your subconscious will agree. I once heard that the human brain is a wonderful screen. It will only let you desire things you are capable of achieving. You'll never desire anything you're not capable of doing. Some of these will require a great deal of work. Whether you're ready to put forth the effort or not, that's another story. That's a powerful thing to know. Even more powerful is selecting a time each year to update your goals, such as Christmas, New Years, your birthday, or another special time for you.

Your list of goals should be a living document; and when you start desiring something new, the list will need adjusting. Yes, it is okay to drop goals. As you mature in goal setting, you will find that some goals will waste your time and effort. You could achieve them but at too high a price. In order to achieve your goals, you must take the time to define them, review them, and believe in them.

Achieving your goals sometimes comes with a new set of problems. Let me give you an example. Remember, I wrote that I got a deal on a sailboat I couldn't turn down. For years I had "own a sailboat" on my goal list. One of the things I had always done was let my bosses and coworkers know what my goals were.

When I was a Battery Commander at Ft. Hood, Texas my Battalion Commander was selected to attend the War College (proof that awesome teams move you to the top). He called me into his office one afternoon.

I went in, stood at attention, and reported, as I thought I was in trouble. He laughed, "You're not in trouble. Sit down. I'm going to help you achieve one of your goals."

Relieved, I sat down and asked him which one. He told me he had a sixteen-foot sailboat and didn't want to go through the hassle of taking it with him to the War College. The bottom line was that he offered me a deal on the sailboat that I couldn't refuse. Now for the problem. I had bought a beautiful boat and trailer, but I didn't have a clue how to sail it. It gets even worse. All of my friends knew I wanted the boat so I felt foolish asking them for help. I've had many such dilemmas in my life, but as my minister once said, "Pray for problems." I did learn to sail. A young PFC in my Battery was excited to teach the "Old Man" how to sail.

I feel one more item needs to be addressed under this topic. No one is perfect. As a manager, you must keep that in mind at all times. Your people are going to screw up; expect it and act like a Duck.

9

The Train

There was a little boy that's family had the custom of making a wish list for Christmas. It was a list of things they would like to receive from Santa on Christmas morning. It was a good system and it worked well--**well**, that is until the little boy tried to beat the system. You see, the little boy was a "peeper". He would search until he found his Mom and Dad's hiding places to see what they had bought for him.

One year the little boy discovered a train set and he was very happy! He wanted a train set more than anything in life. Because he was so happy, he made out his list and kept it short (only ten items). To keep it under ten, he left the train set off the list (since he knew he didn't need to ask for it). Christmas morning he was up at daybreak. Guess what he found? No train set. The little boy felt like his life was over. He got plenty of other presents, but no train set.

That afternoon his Mom knew something was wrong. She asked, "Why are you so unhappy?"

With tears in his eyes, the little boy said, "I didn't get the one thing I wanted most."

Mom asked, "What would that be?"

The boy replied, "A train set."

His mom said, "But a train set wasn't on your list."

It wasn't until thirty years later that the little boy learned that his Dad was more excited about getting a train set than his son was. However, because he wanted to make his son happy he returned the train set so he could afford all the other items the son requested. It was a sad Christmas for his Father also.

The moral of this story is: If you don't identify your true goals on your wish list, what wonderful gifts will be taken away from you and your family?

Make a list (write down your goals) and make it a long list!

10

The Operator

The year we celebrated my Dad's 80th birthday was a good year. I was able to watch the construction of the dam built to create Ann's and my three-acre lake.

This gives me an opportunity to provide you a quick lesson on goal setting. Ann's goal (really it was a dream, as she refused to write down her goals) was to have waterfront property. I was very proud of my brainstorm to create a three-acre lake because I had met my sweetie's goal. What I didn't know was that Ann was thinking salt water. So, for the lesson, be sure you have a complete picture of your goal (my excuse was that she refused to write it down, but as you know wives are not very good students; especially of husbands). But I digress…

While I enjoyed watching one of my goals being completed I could not help but notice how the crew worked like a well-oiled machine. One man operated a track hoe, another a ten ton truck, another a large dozer and last but not least a packer. They would come to work at 7 in the morning, take just 30 minutes for lunch and leave at 5 p.m. It was spellbinding to watch them. The truck backed up to be loaded; then when it reached the spot the loader wanted, he blew his horn. When he finished loading he blew his horn again. The driver of the truck took the load of dirt to the dozer operator. The dozer was parked where he wanted the next load dropped. The dozer man then pushed the pile across the dam, increasing its height by about six inches. Then the packer did his job. This went on all day long with zero voice commands. I was impressed.

I made my feelings known to the owner and thanked him for making one of my dreams come true. I also pointed out how impressed I was with the operator of the dozer. The owner told me the story of how the operator was hired. He said that one day the driver had come to him looking for a job.

The owner asked him if he had any experience. The operator answered that he had fourteen years' experience and asked about the pay. The owner paid eight to fifteen dollars an hour based on how well the operator performed. They were on a job site at the time, so the owner directed the operator to get on one of the dozers and show him what he could do. The operator quickly cranked the dozer and cut a path about one hundred yards long. The owner said the path was so rough he was not sure a four-wheel drive vehicle could manage it. On the return trip, however, the roadbed he cut was perfectly level from one end to the other.

When the operator returned he was asked what had happened on the first run. The operator responded, "That was an eight dollar man on the way out and a fifteen dollar man on the way back."

The owner smiled. "The operator of the dozer on your project is the fifteen dollar an hour man, and he's due for a raise."

Think how nice it would be if when you hired people for your team it would be as clear a decision as it was hiring the dozer operator. Another thing that stood out was that his team seemed to be extremely happy, and ran as smoothly as a Swiss watch.

11

Act Like a Duck

My wife Ann keeps a picture on the refrigerator with the following caption: "Always behave like a duck. Keep calm and unruffled on the surface, but paddle like the devil underneath."

I can think of several people this advice applies to, but the first person who came to mind was my Dad. My first memory of Dad behaving like a duck occurred in the summer of 1958. I was a member of the FFA (Future Farmers of America). In our chapter, each new member was given a ten-week old piglet to raise. The requirement was to show the pig at the county fair and when the pig had a litter we were to give one of the piglets to the next new member. This task seems simple enough, but many people are not aware of a pig's intelligence. Along with their intelligence comes considerable stubbornness.

My pig (Betty Ann) did not like staying in her pen. She would break out at least once a month. My youngest sister was thrilled to tell me that my pig was out and needed to be put back in the pig lot. One hot August day, Betty Ann escaped by digging under the fence. My little sister did nothing to stop her but was quick to let me know when it happened. The chase began. You would be surprised just how fast a pig can run. Betty Ann cut through a small blackberry patch with me right behind her. When I cleared the last briar something stung me near my temple. I took off the green cap I was wearing and it immediately turned to bright yellow. Miss Betty Ann had just led me through a yellow jacket nest. My legs were completely covered. I raked my hands over my legs killing a hundred at a time. Escaping this area seemed to be the appropriate approach. I ran to the house shedding my clothes as I ran.

Standing inside in just my jockey shorts, I tried to explain to Mom why I had so many stings. She became hysterical because the nearest hospital was twenty miles away.

Dad heard the uproar and came out to see what all the commotion was about. He took one quick look and went to the tool shed. He brought me a garden hoe and pointed to the lower part of our garden. "Go hoe the last two rows of corn and make sure you cut all of the weeds."

His reaction took me completely by surprise. I stomped off down to the field and began hoeing and talking to myself. *"He hates me. I am going to die from all these stings, and all my Dad wants is his corn taken care of."* The more I hoed the madder I got and the madder I got, the harder I worked. Soon I began to sweat. The more I sweated the less the stings hurt. Within an hour all of the pain and soreness was gone. Of course, I must have been a sight to see hoeing the corn in my jockey shorts. Years later Dad told me he nearly panicked when he saw me with all of those stings, knowing the hospital was so far away. However, sweating had once helped him with a couple of stings so he thought it would work for me.

His approach and appeal to me illustrate calm guidance. I did not see his inner panicky feeling as he started paddling like the devil. Over the years I have known and worked for a lot of Ducks. They all have many of the same characteristics. First, they know what they want done. More importantly, they know what could knock them off track. They believe action is the best teacher. They make a decision, they take action, they look at the results and they learn. Lessons learned are applied to their next action and so on and so on. This type of person seems to have all the confidence in the world. However, when they let you into their decision-making process you find out their minds are paddling like the devil. They know what they want to accomplish. They go after it. The one characteristic I have seen in all the ducks I've worked for is they never show emotions, no matter how excited you are when you tell them the world is about to end. Their calmness has always made me feel they will give me the solution. I have tried to grow to their level of confidence. I challenge you, as a manager, to seek that level of competency.

Don't be afraid to try. What's the old saying? ***Fake it until you make it***. If you refuse to take the challenge and plan on being successful, you have big problems ahead of you. Yet, ***the more successful you are the more problems you will have.*** If you panic or lose your temper every time you hear bad news, guess what? Soon you will never hear bad news from your people. Honestly, would you want a manager that didn't know what's going on around him? See how many days it takes for you to become a duckling. Wouldn't it be great if all of our leaders were ducks?

12

Pray for Problem

When I was a small boy, I attended a church service that made a lasting impression on me. A senior member of the church had been buried that week. The minister was commenting on what he had heard at the funeral. People were telling his widow that Brother Bob is problem-free now. The minister shared how Bob had done more than his fair share of problem solving in his 92 years. He was amazed that he had been the happiest man he had ever known. This was true even on his deathbed. No matter how large or small the challenge, he attacked it with enthusiasm. To make a long sermon short, he concluded by saying solving problems is a big part of life. A great part. Start praying for problems if you want to be happier.

Throughout my life I have observed how people handle problems. Many just sit around and complain about how many they have and how life is not fair (not very successful people). The more successful people tend to search out problems and address them promptly.

This is a quality I have observed in people, regardless of age, who excel in whatever they do. They plan for success, looking and asking what obstacles may slow them down. The ability to solve problems is a quality that all businesses seek.

One of my old bosses was always saying, "We do not need problem identifiers. We need problem solvers." People in business for themselves will have many challenges. The more successful they are the more obstacles they will need to overcome. Some people call them workaholics but it's just the opposite for them; they love the challenges. It's like a game. The more they play and the more difficult the situation, the more they like it.

I now see that Bob discovered this secret early in his life and I only regret that I didn't know him better. He was a very successful man even after death. What a wonderful example Bob set for anyone who knew him.

Remember, pray for problems, especially in your business, and then hire more people to help solve those problems so they can share in your success. The more successful you are the more problems you'll have.

This is the reward for being successful.

13

Miracle Plant

My miracle plant is gone! According to Webster's Dictionary a miracle is an event or effect in the physical world deviating from the known laws of nature. What made my plant so special? Well, I'll tell you.

When Ann and I arrived in Germany a few years ago we observed the farmer next door while he planted cabbage. When he made his turn at the end of the row he dropped several plants on the ground. I retrieved one and planted it in my back yard. My back yard was well shaded; however, I picked the spot that receives the most sun.

The miracle came the first year. The plant grew to about six inches, but it only had a dozen leaves. During the winter it was covered with snow several times, but it survived. The second year it grew two more inches, lost all its old leaves and grew four more. It survived another snowy winter and in its third year it grew two more inches.

Well, not everyone recognizes a miracle when they see it. I hired a gardener to work in my yard. Not recognizing how special this plant was, the gardener cut the plant, thinking it was a weed.

I have been thinking about my little miracle cabbage plant ever since. Somewhere I heard that a miracle usually teaches a lesson.

What lesson should I have learned? The cabbage plant did not mature because of a lack of sunshine, but it survived the winter—that was in the good Lord's territory!

As I thought about it more I began to remember other miracles in my life. Many were results of goals accomplished. Many of my friends also shared miracles that made their dreams come true. The lesson we should learn from the little cabbage plant is this: Just as it never was able to achieve maturity due to insufficient sunlight, many will never experience the miracle of dreams-come-true because they never take the time to write down their goals. *A man without written goals is like my cabbage plant without enough sunshine. He may grow old but will never reach his potential.*

14

Desire

I was watching a movie about the track star Pre Fountaine when I heard something that reinforced a personal belief of mine. The young runner was not completely motivated to run his upcoming race in the 1980 Olympics. The coach looked him in the eyes and said, "**I can coach anything but desire**. If the desire is not there you are going to lose." He knew the other runners did not have Fountaine's talent or strength, but they would win because of their desire. Pre Fountaine came in fourth.

Desire is defined in the dictionary this way: to express a wish for. **I define desire as life changing when a goal is achieved.** Desire resides deep within your soul. It can be a major driving force. Achieving desires, in my opinion, is the quickest way to building self-esteem. High self-esteem is the birthplace for new desires.

Why do people fail to achieve their "**burning desires?**"

In most cases "**desire killers**" put out the fire. Desire killers are all around us. Most of them can be found among our own family members and friends. I am not sure the desire killers actually do the killing consciously. A careless word or comment will stop a desire or dream in its tracks. For example, a young child tells Dad that he wants to be a writer when he grows up. Dad replies, "How can you expect to be a writer when you only make C's in English?" The dream of being a writer is gone. However, this may not be the worst thing that happened. From that moment on the child may not share his dreams with Dad or anyone else. If he doesn't share them, they will not get shot down, but will he believe in them himself?

You must guard against imposing your non-desires on your fellow man. Fight yourself when you want to tell a friend that skydiving is stupid. Did he try to make *you* jump? The majority of the time when people share their desires they are looking for a simple, "**You can do that.**"

Why is it so hard for us to help someone when they need to overcome the "doubt" obstacle? Desire killers can be very self-righteous when it comes to spreading their influence.

Every day can be the start of a new year and a new attitude. Stomp out the "Desire Killers" in your life. This will be a major paradigm shift. Start verbalizing your true desires. **Don't fool yourself**. When did you stop telling people what you want to be when you grow up? What do you really desire? Tell me. Tell everyone. Seek support from your family and friends. Point out to them when they are being desire killers. Many times they are not aware they are being so destructive. Ask them why? Why would you want to kill someone's dreams?

What if Edison didn't have a hearing problem? What if he could have heard all of those desire killers? I heard that it took him over 10,000 attempts to find an element for the light bulb. That kind of persistence can only come from believing in your dreams. I would like to leave you with this thought.

Just how many dreams have you killed? If you cannot support someone's dreams, at least fight the urge to kill their dreams.

15

Destination Disease

My first real vision began in the eighth grade. My buddies and I liked to play a game we called war. We built our paper Armies in class when we were supposed to be studying. We fought the war during recess. There were five of us – I'll call them Joe, Tom, Bill, Eddie and Pat (me). The real guys may not want their families to know they were goofing off in the eighth grade. We fought this ongoing war until spring. Why did we stop? Well, the eighth grade class had a spring dance. That meant we had to learn to dance with a girl (war didn't seem quite so important anymore), but I digress…

When we weren't fighting the big battles, we talked about what we were going to do when we grew up. Three of us had developed a vision (a big picture of our life). Joe was going to be a policeman, Bill was going to be a Marine like his older brother, and I was going to be a Second Lieutenant in the Army.

Tom and Eddie had no plans for the future. Well, my vision as a Second Lieutenant came true. Bill died a Marine in Viet Nam and Joe retired a few years ago as a police detective in DeKalb County. Eddie never left his family's farm and I'm sorry to say Tom died in prison.

I, however, fell victim to **destination disease**. This can occur anytime one reaches a desired goal or position in life. After I suffered through the disease, I began to recognize its symptoms in others around me. For example, have you ever heard people say, "Bob peaked in high school"? He may have been the star quarterback of the football team and still lives on those glories today. It's apparent that at one time he had a major goal, and that was to be the quarterback of his high school team. When he accomplished that goal he never came up with another vision. He could spend the rest of his life with destination disease.

When I made Second Lieutenant, I went the next seven years without a new vision, and therefore, just took life as it came. When I was about to turn thirty I worried myself into a high temperature along with severe pains in my stomach.

Doctors told me it was only my nerves and that I was in perfect health. I was attending school at the time and the doctor thought I was worried because the final exam was the next day. I knew that I was concerned that life was going to pass me by and I would miss it. That weekend I began to look for another vision – a vision that would bring passion back into my life. I turned thirty in the early seventies and that's when I came up with **rule # 4: Don't fool yourself.**

At that time, I also got truly serious about annually updating my goals. The more visions I had the more successes I had. And with the successes, I had bigger visions. People often complain about lack of time, when a lack of direction is the real problem. Vision gives people direction and confidence.

16
Rule # 4: Don't Fool Yourself

I just admitted I was thirty years old before I made **"Don't Fool Yourself"** one of my rules. (Tell me I'm not a slow learner). It is always easy to recognize when someone else is fooling himself or herself. For some reason it's not so easy if you're doing the same thing. An easy example is the college student saying his course load is too heavy, so he decides to drop out of school for a couple of semesters and come back when he has a fresh mind. Everyone except him knows that without a life tragedy or something else causing him a major paradigm shift, he will never return to school.

I used to fool myself by saying that one day I was going to get organized. My wife has known for years that that will never happen. I don't fool myself anymore about that. No, I didn't get organized; in fact, the closest I got to being organized was to know which pile the item I was looking for was in.

When I did admit I had this little fault I hired an AA who was extremely organized. What surprised me the most when I hired her was that she really enjoyed organizing things? Who knew there were people like that?

17

Sharpening Your Tools Is Never a Waste of Time!

Someone sent me an article from the hometown newspaper in Tennessee about my granddaughter, and it started me thinking about how lucky I was to be raised near my grandparents. My Father's parents only lived a quarter of a mile from us. My grandfather retired from "the plant" when I was about thirteen. He threw himself into improving his 100-acre farm. My grandfather (or Papaw, as I called him) was a big man with an even bigger temper. He was without doubt the most stubborn person in our family. Ann tells me I must be his grandson. Life was always exciting around Papaw. He and Mamaw had 9 children, 6 boys and three girls. The two youngest sons were only four to six years older than me. They were often the victims of Papaw's anger.

I remember once while I was watching him replace the white oak shingles on the smoke-house is how his temper overcame him.

He had spent all morning cutting the shingles from a large white oak and was getting tired. He started to replace some of the old shingles and hit his thumb instead of the nail. Anger took hold of him and he threw that hammer as far as he could. As tired as he was, he had the strength to throw the hammer a great distance. He then took a break. After resting and drinking some water he returned to the task.

In the midst of anger, he had forgotten what he had done with the hammer. He began to yell at his wife, **"Mandy, those God Blame boys hid my hammer again."**

"God Blame" was his favorite curse word. My grandparents had been married for fifty years so Mandy didn't even answer. I saw where the hammer had landed and quickly retrieved it for him. He blushed and said, "Don't tell your Mamaw." He then said, "Come over early tomorrow and we'll make that bow I promised you."

I was there before he could finish breakfast the next morning, and that was early since he ate breakfast before daybreak. I got excited when he said we needed to cut a hickory log to make the best bow. We went to the tool shed to get the axe. Then immediately Papaw started back towards the house and I thought I would die. I asked him where he was going and he responded, "To get a file to sharpen the axe."

I told Papaw that sharpening the axe was going to waste too much time.

His response was, **"Sharpening your tools is never a waste of time."** Sure enough, thirty minutes after we entered the woods Papaw had cut and split a small hickory tree. When we returned to the workshop he started to work with his sharp drawing knife. Two hours later I was the proud owner of a five-foot bow that would send an arrow over 100 yards. I thought I was "Robin Hood" of the north Georgia mountains.

For many years I only used this "sage" advice on my hand tools. Then I realized that listening was also a tool. So are goal setting, team building and salesmanship. When I learned about alternative choices, I thought I'd found the coolest tool around. "Sir, would you like an appointment on Monday or Thursday? Morning or afternoon?" No was not an option.

I decided to try this new tool on the toughest nut possible, my five-year old son, Michael. That night after dinner I asked him, "Michael, do you want to take a shower or a bath?" He answered, "Bath." "Do you want it before this television show or after?" "Before." Then he ran upstairs to the bathroom. I asked my wife what she'd done with my real son. She was just as shocked as I was. I knew I now had a razor sharp tool.

18

Trust

While living in Germany I made a point of flying home each year for my Dad's birthday. When I was home for his 79th I wandered up to my grandparents' old homestead. I began to reminisce about my wonderful childhood with Papaw and Mamaw. I told you about his temper and his awesome respect for sharp tools. Another event came back to me while I was at home that I had almost forgotten. My grandfather was a man who believed his word was his bond. Once he decided a person couldn't be trusted, he would have nothing to do with them.

I need to point out he was also strong-willed and stubborn. Knowing this, you'll appreciate his reaction to Neil Armstrong becoming the first man to walk on the moon. I was away at college when the moonwalk took place.

I came home the next weekend and could hardly wait to talk to Papaw and Mamaw about the historical event. I had the shock of my life when Papaw said, "Son, you don't believe they really went to the moon, do you? They just made a movie and put it on TV. Our government is made up of crooks and liars and they could never do something that hard."

"But Papaw, I do believe we really landed men on the moon," I said.

He insisted, "Trust me, son, it's just a big lie. They never actually do anything."

I'm not sure what caused my grandfather to develop such a total lack of trust for our government; however, he died 8 years later still believing the moon landing was just another sham by the government.

My father has similar strong feelings about trust and I suppose I do, too. Let me ask you: Do you work for a company based on trust? What is trust anyway? My feeling is that another word for trust is dependability. Trust is doing the right thing simply because it's the right thing to do.

True trust is knowing that if we give someone our word we will perform or die trying. It also means that if one of the team members makes a promise, the rest of the team will make sure it isn't broken. The difference in an awesome team and just a group of workers is the can boss trust in them. Can he depend on you and your team?

There are more people than you believe who respond as my grandfather did. You can only lose your honor or trust once with them. I like to compare trust to a fragile Christmas tree ornament. Once it's broken, there is no way you can repair it.

19
Team Building

The most important step in team building is the **vision.** If there's no vision, nothing will ever be accomplished. What do I mean by **vision**? My definition of vision is a **goal** so big that you need help (or a team) to make it happen.

If you are the leader of your team, your role is to do what only you can do: **keep painting the big picture for your people**. As the leader building a successful team, you can never forget that every person on the team has a role to play and every role plays its part in contributing to the **vision.** Without this perspective the team cannot accomplish its goal.

I need to give you a caution. Remember**, it's your vision.** The mere accomplishment of this vision is a sufficient reward for you, but it is not a sufficient one for your team members. To them, this is only an objective and they need rewards, motivation and incentives. That requires you to break the vision down into milestones and time frames.

The nice thing about this step is that you don't need to do it by yourself. Let the team help. In fact, if the team sets the milestones they will develop ownership of the process.

As you get new team members in, you must educate them on where the team has been, where they are now, and what the team is trying to achieve. Most importantly, you need to let the team member know how he fits into the scheme of things. Many leaders fail in this step. They assume that the new person will pick up what needs to be done. Not telling a team member what is expected of him is the number one reason teams fail.

As your team grows, you'll soon realize you need help. That help is called an office manager. As a district manager I was lucky enough to find an awesome one. By that time I had already learned the art of delegating and that turned out to be a plus. The more I delegated, the more she took control. I can't take credit for her training as she'd been an office manager in a sister district overseas. Her husband was in the Army and had been assigned to a post near my office. My old office manager was also a military spouse.

Her husband had been given orders to Germany. When I called the district manager there looking for a job for my old office manager, my friend was delighted. His response was that we'd just trade. The first words out of my new office manager's mouth as she walked through my door were, "Mr. Patterson, I think I work for you."

Let's begin with where do you find talented, independent, motivated and educated assistants? That is an easy answer. If you live near a military post, no problem. You are looking for a military spouse. Because the military moves their soldiers every three to four years, it's almost impossible for their spouses to find quality jobs. Don't be surprised to find you're interviewing a spouse that has a masters or even a Ph.D. I even had one office manager who was a member of MENSA. I didn't find out how truly smart she was until my first training meeting. So the short answer is to hire a military spouse.

There's good news and bad news. The good news is they are smart, educated and because many of their partners are away fighting wars they become independent, flexible and fearless.

The bad news is they will leave you in three years. A good office manager is like a good First Sergeant. It's like they read your mind and complete tasks before you even know you have a problem. An office manager is the mainspring in your Swiss watch. One thing they do that you will appreciate immensely is they know the true feelings and concerns of all the AAs in the office. The most important part is that she will tell you when you need to know.

20
Delegate

With the passing of the years I have come to realize just how lucky I was to grow up on a small farm. I say small because it wasn't large enough to support our family. My father had to work at the "plant" to keep us fed and clothed. He did a quality job. Because he worked all day, there were many tasks that fell to the children on the farm. They were referred to as "chores". Parents today do not realize what a powerful tool "chores" can be (and legal torture for their children). Can you believe our parents really expected us to do chores every day and on time? (How cruel). I'm not sure what I learned from chores. I will address that another day.

It was the "other tasks" and how my Father approached them that taught me a most powerful leadership lesson. As I sit here and write these notes, I'm amazed at how much my Father respected and trusted me.

Respect and trust are what you need to **delegate** a job to another person and let him or her perform that job without your interference. I was just entering my teens when Dad began to give me "new jobs." He would describe the new task something like this: "Son, the cow has gotten out and is in Bonnie Evans' cabbage." That cow loved cabbage, especially Bonnie's. "Go get her and fix the fence. Oh, and tell Bonnie we'll pay her for the cabbage."

You may ask: "What was so powerful about those directions?"

Saying "No" to Dad never entered my mind, especially since I didn't know who he blamed for the cow getting out. I knew immediate actions were in order. Let me tell you just what the simple directive entailed. First, we lived on a 200-acre farm with almost 60 acres in fences. There was one big area that was mostly wooded. The cattle could roam anyplace they wanted and hopefully return to the barn at night. Because most of the fence was in the woods, falling trees and limbs were a constant problem.

When Dad said, "Fix the fence," he might as well have said, "Mission impossible," because that's what it meant to me. In my thirteen-year-old mind I was wondering, *just how did the cow get out?* The first thing I did was run and check all of the gates. They were closed and locked. I then checked the entire fence line near Bonnie's house. No luck. About two hours later I found the break. When my father built the fence he had used an old oak tree as a corner post. During one of our summer storms the oak fell and took down almost fifty feet of wire along with the broken post. I have to say, finding the break in the fence was the easy part compared to what came next. After six freshly dug postholes, six cut posts, and fifty feet of newly strung wire, the problem was solved.

The King of Accountability, my Dad, asked the next weekend where the fence was broken. I proudly announced the old oak at the spring had blown over. Eagerly I was prepared to tell him how much work that old tree had caused when he said, "I guess you should cut it up for firewood next week." New task.

I cannot believe how much trust my Dad had in me. He knew I had never dug a posthole before, much less cut posts and string wire. I did not even know how deep to dig. It was a good thing the old oak pulled one of the posts out of the ground. I hoped the old post was the correct depth because that was the measurement I used. Dad never gave me the feeling that I was not up to the task. I will never forget how proud I was when telling Mom in detail what I did. I certainly hope Mom shared all of her secrets with Dad because I could never thank him enough for his guidance.

My father's trust and high expectations taught me to delegate and trust my subordinates. This was especially effective in my military career. One of my mentors, Dave Thoreson, reinforced this lesson. He always said, **"People will always rise to your expectations!"**

Good leaders and managers learn to delegate. It takes a strong leader to trust employees to do their jobs. When everything goes great, it's easy; however, the real test is when it doesn't.

It may take all your strength but you must fight the urge to step in and do or supervise the task. If you can stand back and let your employees resolve the problem, the task may not be up to your standards initially; however, the employee will respond to your trust and encouragement. I've found a little trust will turn an apathetic worker into a future team leader – an employee that you no longer need to supervise. If you trust them, be patient. You will develop a team that will take you to the top.

21

Team Communication

The success of your team and the ability of the team members to work together are completely dependent on good communication. Everyone involved needs to learn to develop this skill in a couple of areas.

First, from you to your teammates. I believe everything rises and falls on leadership. Leadership rises and falls on communication. A good leader is consistent. Nothing frustrates team members more than a leader who cannot make up his mind. I always referred to my four rules to make my decisions easier.

1. **Establish goals**

2. **Take care of your teams and friends**

3. **Don't get greedy**

4. **Don't fool yourself**

In addition: Be clear. Your team members cannot excel if they don't know what you want. Don't try to dazzle them with your intelligence, rather impress them with your straightforwardness.

As they say in the Army: **KISS** (Keep it simple, stupid**).** Try to seek the easy solution. It is a mistake for a leader to look for an exotic solution as a way of trying to impress his or her team members. Simple is best and is the easiest to explain. Another plus is it's usually the fastest route to the solution. Law # 12: **When you have a problem, think horses not zebras.**

Be **courteous.** Everyone deserves to be shown respect. Never forget that because you are the leader, your communication sets the tone for the entire team. Knowledge is only power if you show it. Teams always reflect their leaders.

Second, from the team to you. The best leaders listen, invite and encourage participation. Competent leaders never want 'yes' men. They want direct and honest communication from all team members. I will steal a good idea no matter where I hear it. (Plagiarism is only bad in school; in any other context, imitation is the sincerest form of flattery.)

Teams succeed or fail based on the way members communicate with one another. Interaction fuels action. That's the power of communication.

22
Learn to Listen

Have you ever thought you were so right about something that you went into the "telling mode" and refused to listen? The end result was embarrassment and total loss of control of the entire situation.

A few years ago I was assigned to work as an Army National Guard advisor in Long Beach, California. In the process of getting settled, I visited the local K-Mart about two blocks away. I had been in the store about ten minutes when a gentleman approached me and addressed me by name.

"Captain Patterson?"

I answered, "Yes, but I'm an LTC now."

Come to find out, we had served together in Vietnam and he was now in the National Guard unit I was advising. Small world!

About three months later I was once again in the same K-Mart when I observed a gentleman in the stationary department who looked very familiar. I approached him and said, "I'm sorry, I can't seem to remember your name but I am sure that we have served together."

I went on to tell him I was in the Army and was now working as a National Guard Advisor. He politely said he had served in the Navy. I kept talking. I told him the only time I had worked with the Navy was during Vietnam. He told me he had never served there. He told me about how he had made a lot of friends and traveled to many other countries while in the military. We decided that a requirement for the US Senate should be to visit a third-world country. Our conversation went on for about thirty more minutes, until I could **tell** no more.

I then said, "It looks like we never served together, but I never forget a face."

The man looked up from the notebook he was holding and said, "**I'm Alex Haley**."

The fireworks went off in my head. This man was the famous author of **Roots.**

Embarrassed can only begin to describe how I felt. I immediately, and I do mean immediately, said apologetically, "I'm sorry, Mr. Haley."

As I scurried toward the exit, I heard him say, "Thanks for reminiscing."

My first thought was to get as far away as I could. Distance did not help. It took years before I admitted meeting Alex Haley, much less how I had forced him to retrace his military career. The lesson I learned was to listen. This experience was most helpful to me when I conducted interviews with potential employees

Before I met Alex Haley I would never have listened for them. Before Haley I would TELL, TELL and never know if the man would be a good hire.

Have you met your Alex Haley? By now you can see I usually learn everything the hard way. Whatever it takes for you to learn the art of listening, do it. I cannot think of anything more important.

23

Take Care of Your teams and Friends

What's that old saying? To have a friend, you must be one. What is a friend? Most friends I have observed over my lifetime are the ones who sincerely listen to what you are saying. I have also noticed that usually one of them is a better listener than the other. This sometimes forces the listening friend to find his own sounding board. Over the years I've seen people get their feelings hurt when they find out that their close friend has an even closer relationship with someone else. Think about your own friendships. Are you the talker or the listener? **Don't fool yourself.** Only you will know the answer, so be truthful with yourself. If you're the talker, try listening more. Listening will require you to ask questions. Listen with both your eyes and ears.

I was lucky I learned the listening lesson while in the military. When I became a financial planner, my skills as a listener were my best asset.

Pat Patterson's definition of a friend is someone who knows all the bad stuff about you and still likes you. When working with clients on their financial future you are forced to ask some very personal questions. If there's any bad stuff, they don't hesitate to tell you. This has a good side and a challenging side. The good side is they will tell you what their dreams are. I would help them change their dreams to goals with a written plan. The challenging side is that by being nonjudgmental they quickly look at you as a close friend. Remember, a good friend is a good listener. The end result would be that my client began to ask my opinions on matters other than financial business.

Most of my clients at that time were young, military officers. Now I had a twenty plus years military career, but I seemed to give more guidance to these young Lieutenants and Captains than I ever did on active duty. I'm proud to say that it turned out to be very beneficial to me. I've received a lot of **warm fuzzes** over the years. I still receive notes, phone calls and cards from those young officers and their families. Of course, they're now Colonels and Generals. I feel those **warm fuzzes** are some of my best achievements.

24

Shortcuts

Over the years I have observed people trying to save time and money by taking what they thought was a shortcut. In the end, someone always had to clean up the mess. I remember when I was just a kid on the farm and was hoeing corn with my sisters. The primary purpose of the task was to cut the weeds so the corn could get a better start. We hated this job. The older of my two sisters quickly discovered that by reaching out two feet with the hoe she could cover a lot more ground and get to the end of the row faster. Actually she was cutting the weeds as the hoe went into the ground and covering the ones near her feet with the loose dirt. When you observed her work, it looked great; however, in about three days the weeds she failed to cut grew twice as fast as the corn.

As the oldest child, I was given the task of redoing those rows.

Looking out over the fields it was easy to see which rows needed hoeing. I guess this technique worked for my older sister because my younger sister and I would not let her into the field after this incident. This was my first lesson and experience in cleaning up after someone else who took a shortcut. My older sister was the real loser in this situation, as she never got to feel the pride in a job well done. My younger sister still talks about cleaning those cornrows.

One of my agents took a shortcut on a client's annual financial review. He felt it was a waste of his time to review the client's file before he came in. After five years as an agent he was sure he could answer any question his client might ask. This client had recently married and wanted his new wife to understand their financial plan. Trust me, he was an ideal client. Now, here's the bad news. The client died six months later. The agent gave me a panicked call. Because of his shortcut, he had overlooked the fact that the client's father was still the beneficiary of his insurance policy – not his new wife. She wouldn't even have enough money to pay for his funeral.

If this wasn't bad enough, instead of learning from his mistake he continued to take shortcuts and move to the investment side of financial planning. His shortcuts came back to haunt him: at 40 years of age he lost his job. I understand he now hangs sheetrock for a living.

25

The Chicken

When I was about ten years old I found an old table knife in the trash. I began to play Indian and practiced throwing until I could stick it in the ground almost every time. I then started to find targets – cans, boxes, etc.--anything I thought the knife would penetrate. As my skill improved my confidence improved and I became a little cocky. That's when the stupid boy came out again.

We lived on a small farm. We had cows, horses and pigs, but no chickens. My father hated chickens, but his brother Bud, whose farm joined ours, loved them. The problem was that he let them run free and sometimes they wandered over to our house. I'm not sure what came over me, but one afternoon a big, white chicken came within eight feet of me while I was standing on the back porch. Without thinking, I threw the knife at this innocent chicken and as with the cans and other items, I hit the target.

The knife hit her neck just below her head and she dropped like a sack of flour. My younger sister, old big mouth, saw the killing blow and couldn't wait to tell my Father.

I'll never forget the first words that came out of his mouth. "How much money have you saved, son?"

Surprised at the question, I answered, "One dollar and twenty-seven cents." At that age you know to the penny how much you have.

With his arms folded across his chest he said, "Go get it and take it to Bud. Tell him you killed his chicken and ask if that's enough to pay for it."

I did as I was told.

Over the years we had made a footpath from our house to Bud's. I wouldn't say I was walking slowly, but as my grandmother used to say, "You needed to drive up a stake to see if he was moving." I was about a hundred yards from Bud's house when I was shocked to see my dead chicken come running into his yard.

I could see a blood stain on her neck, but otherwise, she looked healthy. I turned and set a record on getting from Bud's house to ours. Dad saw me coming. He asked, "What did he say?"

I was so excited it was all I could do to talk. I finally conveyed to Daddy that the chicken was okay and had beaten me back to Bud's.

Going back to his normal stern stance, he asked the legendary question, "Did you learn anything?"

"Yes. Leave Bud's chickens alone."

As I think back over my life, this was my first lesson in cause and effect. Over the years I've had many chicken flashbacks when I start to react before thinking first. Remembering that chicken playing possum saved me from many future embarrassments.

26

Smell the Roses

More than 50 pages back I wrote about how the **Yeses** change our lives, not the **No's**. I told the story of how I met Ann. This is a continuation of that wonderful story.

It amazes me how much my life has changed since I met that 5'6" gray- haired lady. She tells me I have taught her many things and changed her life also. I'm not sure if these were for the better, so I don't push it by asking what or how. What's that old saying? "If it ain't broke, don't fix it." I could list many, many positive changes she has produced in me, but today I will address only one. She has taught me to enjoy today – this hour— this minute.

When I think back to B.U. (before us) I was living for the future. Someday I would do that, visit those, enjoy friends, etc., etc. Many people say, "Take time to smell the roses."

Well, to do that you need to slow down and consciously smell them. I now catch myself saying, "Life doesn't get any better" or "You know, I'm having a good time." I try each day to identify what is special and just enjoy it for the moment. Some days I need to look hard, but I always find something.

I feel that Ann has given me a very special gift. I guess this would fall under **"Don't get greedy." We work so hard to get more that we fail to enjoy what we have.**

27

Don't Get Greedy

This rule is a lot deeper than it appears on the surface. Let me approach this from a logical standpoint. In a previous pages I wrote **if the mere accomplishment of the task is reward enough to you, it's a bonafide goal.** I've often wondered why a team leader often wants to take all the credit and applause away from teammates when a goal is accomplished. In my view, **that's pure greed.** Believe me, two minutes of applause is not worth losing the respect of your team.

When I was working on my MBA, the number one reason small businesses failed was that they failed to plan for success. I'm sure that's still true today. If you don't have plans to reinvest in your business, you should. If you let greed overtake your better judgment you will spend all of your profits. I recommend you set aside 10% of your gross profit to reinvest in the business.

Don't keep it a secret from the rest of the team.

Incentives for your team members are a good investment. For example, ask them what is needed to improve the office environment. Once each month I asked my people what I should buy for the office. I was surprised by their answers. Sometimes it was a new shredder, a plant, a new sign for the outside, or simply a new coffee pot. Spending a little money on such small things paid big dividends in our future.

Greed can take the form of unearned recognition, failing to keep the office machine working, or letting employees argue over who is going to buy something as trivial as soft drinks for a meeting. It sounds crazy when you put it on paper, but it can have a major impact on performance and attitude in the office.

I leave you with **Pat's # 1 law: Cheap people can't think big.**

28

Grow or Die

As an entrepreneur you must realize there is a basic rule you can never forget. Your business is either growing or dying – there is no middle ground. If new agents or advisors know this, it will help them to see they must find one new client each week, every week. What I mean by that is if they find two clients this week, they still need to find one more next week. By following Pat's rule #4, Don't Fool Yourself, they will learn they've got to know their numbers. For example, I knew four or five referrals would get me one new appointment and after I got proficient, two out of those three would become my client. So my numbers really turned out very simple. I needed two referrals a day to get me my two clients a week. I was taught if I wasn't in front of a client I wasn't working. An important lesson for a new agent to learn is that time is like money, it should be spent getting the biggest bang for the buck. I once broke down for my agents their hourly income.

Even my weakest agent would make $100 per hour. The catch was they only made the $100 an hour when they were in front of clients. When not in front of clients they were making zero dollars per hour. That meant their AA's were making more money than they were. Sometimes the simple example is the most effective. Have your agents do the math.

29

Keep Them Hungry

As you get older you begin to think of the lessons you learned in your lifetime. Many change your life, and may have changed others' lives if you had the nerve to apply them. There is one lesson I learned early, but failed to apply until a few years ago. When I was young I loved to hunt. I still do. A friend had the best hunting dogs around. Everyone wanted to be invited to hunt with him and his dogs, myself included. I asked Mr. Jim one day why he kept the dogs locked in a pen and why they were so skinny?

He replied without looking up, "I keep them hungry."

Only hungry dogs work well. If hunters hunt every time they want, the desire decreases and they start to see only the work. When I was young I thought Mr. Jim was cruel. I realize now he was my first example of "tough love" (Not counting my Father).

The lesson I learned is keep them hungry. I see parents violating this lesson all the time. I am speaking from experience. As parents we fall into the trap of wanting our children to have everything that we didn't. We want life to be so much easier than it was for us. In our eagerness to make sure they get what they want, we give it to them and rob them of the satisfaction of earning or achieving it for themselves.

How many times have you seen a child get excited about baseball (or any sport) and the parents did everything they could to give him/her everything he needed to be the best on the team. This could be ok; however, we take on a passion that requires the child to do nothing but be involved in baseball 24 hours a day. After a few short years of being super saturated in the sport the kid loses all interest in the game. He or she becomes interested in something different. Maybe in something that we as parents do not understand and therefore cannot provide structure for, like computer games. The game maker knows how to keep the kids hungry.

As a parent, I failed many times to hold my children accountable because I thought it was too hard. I did not want my children to suffer. They are now grown and have to discover failure and frustration without my help.

I also see how I failed to apply this lesson with my clients when I was an agent. Many times I wanted to show the client how smart I was or how easy it was to become financially independent. I ended up taking away the client's hunger for financial independence. We all know it is not easy and will take at least 25-30 years to achieve. My more successful clients are the ones I kept hungry (I am sorry to say it was not planned). Somehow I was asking the right questions so they developed ownership of the long journey to financial independence. When you are working with your clients, think about it. How can you keep them hungry? Every day ask yourself how you can use client "hunger pains" to motivate them.

. **Pat's law # 11: Keep them hungry.**

30

Rabbit Hunting

While living in Germany, Ann and I frequently took long walks through the farmlands. One day we saw a couple of rabbits. They certainly raised them big over there! I could see why rabbit was on the menu in most of their restaurants. For the hour it took us to make the walk we reminisced about the past. Ann's father loved to hunt; quail was his number one choice of prey. My Father's passion was rabbit hunting. Each year he would train a couple of beagles to hunt. When they came up to his standard as hunters he would sell them and take on two more. As my Dad's gopher, I would drag a rabbit skin through fields, brush and briar patches so the new pups could learn how to track.

To be a good trainer you need to know your dogs as well as the animal you're training them to hunt. My first lesson was on jumping a rabbit. When a hunter or dog jumps a rabbit in a field it will start to run.

The unique thing about them is that if the rabbit is pursued, he will run in a large circle and return within ten yards of where he was jumped. All good rabbit hunters know this and are not too upset if they don't see the rabbit right when it is first jumped. I could always impress my high school classmates when I took them hunting by telling them to stand in a certain place and expect the rabbit to run by them. Many were so surprised to see the rabbit coming back at them that they'd forget to shoot. (Who says we don't have fun on a farm?)

A rabbit running in a complete circle is the ideal situation. Only a good dog can make this happen. For example, if the dog is too slow the rabbit will sit down. When he is jumped again he will start a new circle. The spot may be two hundred yards from the nearest hunter. On the other hand, if you have a big, fast dog he will put too much pressure on it and it will find the nearest hole, ending the hunt. If you're going to have a successful hunt, you need the correct size dog. Many people don't realize that beagles are different sizes ranging from twelve to eighteen inches tall. In North Georgia, twelves or fourteens cannot negotiate the briars or brush fast enough to keep the rabbit moving.

The tallest ones are too fast and will catch him or run him into a hole. My Dad knew how rabbits reacted. With his knowledge he was able to train some awesome rabbit dogs.

By now you are surely asking, "What does training rabbit dogs have to do with managing agents?" As managers, one of your responsibilities is to motivate your agents to excel. To achieve this you need to know how your agents respond to outside influences. I found I had basically two types of agents. One group sought personal recognition. The other looked for team recognition.

Personal recognition agents are the easiest to motivate. Just give them a trophy to shoot for and they are off and running. The second group comprises those who many managers fail to inspire. They cannot believe that these agents will not respond to trophies, trips or other expensive trinkets. I like to say basically that people are looking for **"warm fuzzes"** in their lives. The agent seeking recognition gets **his fuzzes** each time he is number one. After a few years I discovered that the value of the trophy had no bearing on their motivation.

In fact to prove this point, several agents that won trips, hotel rooms, etc. never actually used them. The win by itself gave them the warm fuzzy they needed. I stumbled on a way to motivate the team recognition guys by pure luck. Over the years I had noticed my agents always went through a slump during the summer months. With a little research I identified each of the agents' personal best for July through September (our first production quarter). They were all low – some only a quarter of their yearly personal best. I designed a contest that all ten of my agents could win. I asked each agent to provide me a list of three things under $250 that they'd like to have, but would never buy. I then asked them to provide me a list of two things that their spouse or significant other wanted but would never buy. I increased the limit to under $500. The contest was simple. Each time an agent broke his personal best in July, August or September, I would give him the first item on the list. The second **time**, the second **item.** If they should break their summer quarter personal best, the wife would get her first choice. The results were as I expected. The recognition guys earned at least two of their items.

Even a couple of my team recognition guys earned at least one of their items, but what surprised me was that every agent beat his or her quarterly personal best and earned a spouse or significant other their first choice. For a long time after that I always included such an incentive when I needed to motivate that group.

It was another year before I realized that if I had a reward for the team members I would get the desired results. In fact, I would get better results because the individual members of the team would motivate the leader. With this discovery I began to stack up my own warm fuzzes. **Hint: Managers, if you want to motivate all of your teams, keep your rabbits running.**

31

A Good Scoreboard

"Accountability is not a tool to punish, but a tool to reward and a tool necessary to correct deficiencies. **It's a positive tool." -- President George W. Bush**

If a team is to accomplish its goals, it has to know where it stands. The scoreboard provides a snapshot of the game at a given time. What do you measure on your scoreboard? I have found that fewer items are best. I have seen manager's measure referrals, phone calls, cold calls, prospects, and types of appointments. The problem here is you can be the number one agent in the office on this scoreboard and fail to put any production on the books. I once had a boss that measured the types of appointments per week. He wanted two each of five separate types each week. One week I would meet the requirement for three of the five. He was not happy. The next week I'd meet the two areas I missed the previous week and fail to make the other three. He was not happy.

After six weeks of this, I wasn't happy and was ready to quit. Then we agreed I would give him two checklists per week of new clients. From that time on I gave him at least two, but more often three or four each week. He was now happy; but more importantly, I was now happy. The scoreboard had gone from five areas to one.

As an agent, I learned the disappointment of measuring too many areas. As a regional leader I tried to remember that. The one area I found I had the best results with was personal bests – for both the agents and the districts. Another positive thing of just measuring this area is that everyone can win – not just the top performers. The truth is it's harder for a bottom performer to break their personal best than it is for a top performer. This forces all agents to stretch and improve. The more they win, the more you win.

I sent out a newsletter identifying personal bests by agents and districts by name each month. I stumbled on another phenomenon that surprised me. I found there were two types of agents. One agent and his team played to win. The other agent and his team played not to lose. Let me try to explain.

Each month my newsletter published the scoreboard so all could see. At first I only put the top 50% in the newsletter. One of the administrative assistants of the agents complained that her team was never in the newsletter. I explained that his production was too low to make the cut. She explained to me that's why she wanted it in writing (**good thing I learned to listen**).

Let me tell you what great advice that was. The next month I listed every agent and their production in order from top to bottom. Sure enough her agent was on the bottom of the list. I'd like to say that from then on he was at the top, but it just "ain't" so. I can tell you he was never the bottom agent again. A couple of times he was just two above it, but he was never again on the bottom. He knew the other agents he was competing against and spent a lot of time trying to find out where they all were on their production. He never played to be the big winner. He played to never be on the bottom or never to lose. What he didn't realize was that his total production for the year was almost double. I think it was a bigger surprise to him than it was to me when he won our **Phoenix Award** for the most improved.

One more concern I must share with you. Watch what you ask for, because you just might get it. As a district manager I was constantly looking for ways to improve production. My agents usually found new clients via referrals from current clients and every six weeks we conducted a financial planning seminar. The agents made appointments with the seminar attendees. Looking at the numbers I was pleased with the new client appointments; however, the seminar attendance was declining each month. I was faced with the choice of not doing seminars or coming up with an incentive to improve attendance.

Each agent was averaging six attendees. I wanted to improve the number and I knew I needed for them to stretch. I decided the best member of the team to motivate was the administrative assistant (AA). The contest was simple. For any client attendance above six, the AA would receive a cash award of $50. If the AA's agent had ten attendees, she would get $200. Did it work? You better believe it did!

Most AA's were getting anywhere from $300 to $500 per seminar. Sounds great, huh? I thought so, but one day while listening to an AA talk to a prospect who had called in for an appointment I was shocked. I expected to hear the AA offer alternative choices: "Tuesday or Thursday? Morning or afternoon?" Instead she was informing prospects that we were having a seminar in four weeks and they should attend that first before making an appointment.

I quickly realized the mistake I had made. If she had made the appointment, she would have lost $50. I was asking agents to improve seminar attendance at the expense of normal appointments. After that, anytime I came up with a new contest I would ask two of my senior agents to look it over. I'd tell them what I wanted to achieve, and they'd tell me what I'd be getting by doing it that way. Most of the time I needed to make slight adjustments. How did I resolve the seminar contest? I began to give credit to the AA's for the prospects they made appointments for before the seminar.

I didn't lose, as many AA's already had a count of scheduled appointments before the night of the seminar. That meant any new attendee was money in the AA's pocket. Those were fun times.

Let's look at some precautionary notes as you build a scoreboard.

1. It's **worse** to measure too many things than it is to **measure nothing at all**. Try to keep measured events to less than five.

2. Ensure that each of your scoreboards keep your team **focused on the big picture**. If it isn't, change it. Watch what you ask for—you will get it!

3. Where will you get your data? Will it come from the bottom up (from AA or agents) or from the top down (Region or Home Office)?

Get it from the **source** that is the most **timely and accurate. Don't be surprised if getting this information is the hardest thing you have done as a manger.** Trust me, it's worth the effort.

4. How often do you update the data? I have found that weekly revisions seem to be the best timeframe to get the most from all my teams. If you only update monthly, the information comes after the fact, and you have missed the opportunity to **influence work in progress**.

5. What score do you keep? Is it the right score? As the leader of your team, you have primary responsibility for checking the scoreboard. I found if I posted the updates I could quickly see where we needed improvements.

6. The lack of information will frustrate rather than motivate. You must provide timely scores to your team in an easy-to-read format.

7. Remember why you get the big bucks. You should be causing your team to focus on the mission. If you are not doing it as well as you should, then create a better scoreboard that helps you do it.

32

Avoid a Miserable Job

Last year I was able to spend Christmas with my family and a great time was had by all. One evening we went out to dinner at one of the only two nice restaurants in my small town. Our waitress was a little older than I so she was *really* old. Dad commented that her husband had just died and she had to go to work. I was seeing a typical example I often gave my clients about the pitfalls of not having a financial plan. When my Father talked about how hard her husband had worked his entire life, I was reminded of when I worked as a carpenter in Atlanta, Georgia. I was paid well ($6.00 an hour in 1965) but I always had sawdust in my eyes and splinters in my hands and knees. I digress, as usual…

Once we had a carpentry job at Bell Telephone (before the breakup). We were working in the penthouse suite on the 12th floor. It was a new building so the elevators hadn't been installed yet. The week we were there the elevator company came to install the much-desired elevators. I was watching the workers and observed that three of the four were much older than I (I was in my early twenties at the time so the old guys were probably in their 50's). No matter their age, they had to carry all the equipment and tools up the stairs every day. What depressed me the most was the realization that when these old men could ride the elevator their job would be finished? The next day they would have to move on to a new job in a new building and start climbing stairs all over again. I thought, ***What a miserable job.***

It's clear to me that these men were not goal setters. I can't see them writing on their goal list that they wanted to work hard all their life.

33

Grandfather Clock

What's that old saying? **Necessity is the Mother of invention.** I can truly verify that fact. One of my agent's AA's complained to me that all her agent did was talk. It was apparent to me that her agent had failed to explain to this team member her role and how important it was for her to do well. I explained to her that an awesome team is like a beautiful, old Grandfather Clock. Each part of the clock has a job to do. If one part fails it may not keep time or chime at the appropriate time. I went on to explain to her how her agent was like the hands on the clock – out front where everyone can see them. I pointed out that the only time he is at work is when he is in front of the clients. Like the clock's hands, the only time they are needed is when someone is checking the time of day.

She and the other AA's were like the internal workings of the clock behind the face. They work all the time, but no one ever sees their efforts. They are as necessary as the wheels, the gears and the spring in the big clock. Everyone has to perform well if the machine is to run properly. Like any team, at different times one AA or part of the mechanism is the most important part of the team/clock. She needed to understand that neither the AA nor the mechanism is trying to outshine the others. For example, at noon the old clock chimes twelve times. At that particular time the chimes are the most important part of the clock. But moments later the chimes are the least important.

When the agent makes a sale and picks up a check, then the AA, who is responsible to ensure the paperwork is sent to the insurance and investment company, is the most important team member – much more important than the agent at that particular time. On the other hand, when the insurance policy comes back, the AA who is responsible for notifying the client to pick up their policy is now the number one team member.

I was very pleased when she understood the analogy; in fact, all the AA's did. It really helped them to take ownership of their place on the team. The grandfather clock analogy became part of my training packet in developing a new team. The AA's really began to enjoy the power it gave them – the power to tell their agents when they **were slacking off**. If an agent didn't have an appointment one day, they loved telling him that he hadn't come to work yet. When every team member fulfills and excels in the role best suited for his or her talent and experience, then the team really hums.

The achievement of the whole team makes the agent flourish and the achievement of the agent makes the team flourish. The whole team is truly greater than the sum of its parts.

. **Pat's law # 8: Knowledge is power only when you share it.**

34

Betty Ann

I was once asked to check an eight-man office to see why the morale was so low. It took only one day to identify the problem, but it took me a week to come up with an explanation for my boss on what the problem was. I had to return to my boyhood experiences again.

Remember my FFA pig, Betty Ann? Well, as you can guess, I really petted and pampered that pig. So much so that she would not stand for anyone else to enter her pen. One day while Dad had me doing something else, he noticed that Betty Ann had made a hole in the fence. Seeing that it would only take a hammer and a couple of nails to fix it, he started to work.

Let me give you a little pig knowledge: pigs are unable to turn their heads. What they have to do is to knock their intended victim down and then bite or cut with their tusks. Seeing my Father in her territory, Betty Ann began a long run toward him with the intention of knocking him off his feet.

My Father is a farm boy from way back and he had a great deal of pig knowledge. Squatting down, he heard Betty Ann coming and when she was about three feet away he turned and with one motion hit Betty Ann square on the nose with his hammer. It must have been with a great deal of force because from that day on when my Father approached her pen she would get as far away from him as she could. As Dad walked around in the pen, she walked around on the other side in order to avoid him.

Back to the problem office… What I identified was that the office manager enjoyed and abused her power over the other personnel. The AA's responded just like Betty Ann. As the office manager moved through the office, the AA's would seek locations within the office as far away from her as they could. It's hard to get good production from the administrative staff when they are constantly seeking places to hide.

Betty Ann's fear of my Father presented no new problems. However, the only and best solution for the office manager was to let her go.

It's hard to believe one person could be so destructive to an otherwise awesome team. Question to you managers: Can you recognize a **human hammer**; and better still, can you remove it?

35

Lost Opportunity

Let me tell you a story about attitude and motivation that dates all the way back to Custer's Last Stand. First I have to set the stage. Custer's troops were horse soldiers, not cavalry. The difference is that when horse soldiers fight, they dismount, leaving every fourth soldier as a horse-holder. The other three have to do all the fighting. Another reduction in the soldier's effectiveness was their rifles. If they fired rapidly more than three or four times, the weapons jammed. The worst –and most critical—part was that Crazy Horse knew this. The Indian's fighting style is also important to the story. In order to move up the ladder of respect, an Indian brave was required to count coup. A brave would only touch his enemy, effectively saying, "I could have killed you, but I didn't." The Indians call that counting coup (pronounced 'coo').

Indians felt that anyone could kill his enemy, but only the truly brave could touch him and not have to kill him. The first Sioux warrior to touch an enemy in battle, a coup, could wear a golden eagle feather upright. The second wore an eagle feather tilted left. Vertical stripes on your leggings signified coups. Now for the story…

As Custer's men moved into the fighting position, they kicked up huge dust clouds in the hot, dry countryside. On the initial attack, the Indians' primary objective was killing the horse-holders so that the soldiers could not retreat. Under the command of Crazy Horse, the Indians moved back and forth in front of the troopers, just outside of rifle range. Eventually the soldiers' rifles jammed and the young braves began to count coup. This drove the young soldiers crazy. Many had only been in the army for a few months, and their stress level was high.

About the time it looked as if all was lost, a young officer caught one of the free-running horses and swung into the saddle. He rode into a ravine and made his escape.

Five young braves saw him ride away and began the chase. The soldier had a fast horse and was leaving them behind, so the braves began to drop out until just one Indian, who didn't carry a bow or a rifle, followed him. The last warrior was about to give up his chase when the escaping soldier glanced backward, saw the pursuing Indian, jerked out his pistol and shot himself in the head. The Indian warrior later remarked that he had caught the soldier's horse and rode it for years afterward.

Why do I share this story? Let's look at what happened. The soldier had knowledge, experience, a fast horse and opportunity. Because he had the wrong attitude, he missed being immortalized as the only survivor of Custer's Last Stand. What is the moral of this story? Vincent Lombardi said it best: "The difference between a successful person and others is not a lack of strength, not a lack of knowledge, but rather a lack of attitude." My question to you is: Who will ride your horse because you gave up your life's goals just one step away from achieving them?

36

Time to Start

At this stage of reading my ponderings, setting goals might be of interest to you. What you need to do is start. I have left space below for you to write down 10 of your dreams or goals. It's really simple. What do you want to achieve, own, see, or do in the next 10 years?

1

2

3

4

5

For those of you who want to do awesome things, let's use **Pat's rule # 4: Don't fool yourself**. If it took you more than thirty minutes to think of five goals, you **are not** a goal setter. The good news is you **can be cured.** Dreaming just takes practice. Remember how you used to dream as a kid? Now put the dreams on paper and you're halfway to goal setting. The other half is to decide a time frame. Here is a good place to give you another one of my laws: **# 7: There are no bad goals, just bad timing.** That means it may take you a little longer than you planned to achieve the goal, but achieve it you will. A hint on goal setting: **The only cure for being uncomfortable doing something is to do it until you are**.

My mom gave me the special gift of goal setting. I'm sure she would be pleased that I am passing it on to you. I think you are ready to do a little fine-tuning in the goal setting process. It's human nature to keep everything simple and in its own little box. Because of this, anything we want, we call a goal.

The following lesson teaches you that everything you want to do is not necessarily a goal. Sometimes what you want to achieve is an objective. These are just steps on your way to achieving a desired goal. How do I tell the difference? **If the mere accomplishment of the task is reward enough to you, then that is a bon-a-fide goal.** On the other hand, if you need some type of reward or prize for finishing the task, then that's an objective. Even in the Army, they list steps or objectives. The goal is to win the war and establish peace. The objectives are the battles along the way.

Now go back to your list on the previous page and put a checkmark by each task that you need a reward to accomplish. Items on the list left unmarked are goals. I'll bet your list is really short now. In some cases you might not have a list left at all. If so, overcome your fear, and write down your true goals.

Many of my agents wrote down that they wanted to be in the top ten percent of our company, when their true goal was to get the recognition that the top ten would give them or the leadership position it would earn them.

However, they were afraid to let their peers know that. How could I, as their boss, help them achieve their goals if I didn't know what they were? If you really want to learn the true magic of goal setting; and more importantly, goal getting, remember rule number four. **Don't fool yourself**. Write down what it is that you truly want during your short life here on earth. Then you'll really be on your way to goal getting.

Pat's law # 7: There are no bad goals, just bad timing.

37

Summing Up

I spent a third of my life in the military, a third as a financial planner and the other third as a stupid kid. If I had only known in the first third of my life what I know now, I probably wouldn't be any richer, better looking or have any more personal achievements. But I would have stored up a lot more **warm fuzzes**. The special gift of goal setting provided to me by my mother was a true blessing. I regret not being able to tell her the effect it had on me before she passed away.

Let me make this as clear as I can. After 50 years of goal setting I've learned that if you really desire it, there is no such thing as an unrealistic goal. You may remember where I said the brain is a wonderful screen – it only lets you desire things you are capable of achieving. It may be an unrealistic goal for your boss, friends, spouses, and others because it's not their desire. Therefore, they could never accomplish it. Don't try to change these **nay-sayers**. Just don't include them in your goal setting process.

By walking you through the achievements of the European Region of our financial planning company, I can demonstrate how all the steps I've provided came together. When I was given the wonderful opportunity to lead the awesome European team, I had a major dream. I put this dream in writing and set a time frame. That made it **a goal**. Remember, a goal that is so large that you need a team to make it happen is called a vision; and trust me, I had a vision. My **vision** was to grow the region to twice its size so it could be split into two regions in Europe. We started out with seven districts and thirty-eight agents. My vision was to double that size in five years. I pulled in my seven district managers and shared my dream with them. I didn't fool myself – I knew it was my dream, my vision. It would only be an objective to them. They didn't ask, but I knew they were thinking, **'What's in this for me'**? I explained to them my box theory. As district managers, if they recruited and doubled the size of agents in their districts this should double the amount of district production for the company. That would move them out of the box. When a higher leadership position became available, they would be a top contender for the job.

Also, another phenomenon about a business is when it's growing, it seems everyone is happy. When you have a happy district, you have a productive district. To the person (I don't say man, because half of my managers were women) the managers all took on the challenge.

Now all I had to do was come up with a scoreboard and provide feedback to keep them on track and acknowledge their individual achievements. I created a twelve-page newsletter called "The Euro Express" in which I provided the ranking of each district for production, recruiting and personal bests. Most people in the sales world are very competitive and I discovered that competition against their own personal best was their best motivator.

The results: In three years, not five, we grew to 11 districts and 80 selling agents. During that time the agents and districts established over 360 new personal bests. How's that for measurable progress?

The point I need to make now is that it was a slow process, but it was a continuous one. A lot of times I had to act like the duck and you wouldn't believe how fast my feet were kicking!

This quote was given to me by one of my closest friends, Frances Kuhlbars. She is a human thesaurus for appropriate quotes. When she learned that our region would split, she knew we were accomplishing one of our major goals and she provided me with this quote:

"Where many people go wrong in trying to reach their goals is in constantly looking for the big hit, the home run, the magic answer that suddenly transforms their dreams into reality. The problem is that the big hit never comes without a great deal of little hits first. Success in most things comes not from some gigantic stroke of fate, but from simple, incremental progress." -- Andrew Wood

Mr. Wood describes us to a tee. We never had the big hit; however, my scoreboard showed that we put someone on base every month.

We got frustrated in the months that were weaker than the months before, but what many of us didn't realize was that we had improved over the same month the previous year. We were getting better and better – moving our batters around the bases to home plate. Our standards and expectations continued to grow.

All this happened because there was a vision. That vision was written down as a goal, and then communicated to all the agent teams. My question to you is: "**Is your goal written down?** If so, **have you shared it with someone you trust and respect**? If not, stop trying to play the game without a team. Wake up the stored potential that is just waiting to be realized. **Life is a journey not a destination**. Enjoy every step by goal setting all the way.